Lost In The Land Of Kachoo

Written by Tina Scotford

Illustrated by Frans Groenewald

JACANA

Late one morning in the land of Kachoo
A little voice cried out, "What am I to do?
I can't see my mom, I can't see my dad
I can't see my family! Am I going mad?"

The voice belonged to a zebra foal
With sad black eyes, blacker than coal

"How can it be that I'm all on my own?
I need some help," went his soft, little moan

"I'll try and be of valuable help,"
Offered a rhino calf, to stop zebra's yelp
"My eyesight isn't all that good
In fact, it's very, very bad
But together we'll look
to find your mom and dad"

"I think I see them near the tree with the flower
Or are those giraffes, in their group called a tower?
Their coats are orange and splattered with patches
Compared next to yours, I don't think it matches"

Again rhino looked at the tree he had seen
And there sat a young eagle with eyesight so keen

Eagles can look at a very wide range
Which little white rhino found perfectly strange

"Eagle, please lend us a helping hand
By flying overhead and searching the land

We'll stay here and find somewhere to hide
In case we meet up with a lion pride"

Eagle flew up, high with the wind
And for the very first time little zebra foal grinned

"Maybe we can wait with the antelope herd
Until we hear back from our new friend, the bird?
Or maybe we should crouch close to the ground
And listen out for a predator's sound?"

But as they moved forward, nearing a tree
There lurked an animal rhino thought he could see
"Is that your dad with the round black spots?"

"I have stripes! Do you see these as dots?
Your eyesight must be really bad
If you think that leopard is my dad!

We'd better stay very far from that tree
Or else the leopard will dine on me!"

Quietly they snuck down to the river
When the zebra asked, with a shake and a shiver
"Perhaps we should hide among the hippopotami bloat
And jump in the water and lie there and float?

Maybe a hippo I could mistakenly be
But my black and white coat will a predator see

I'll feel so much safer waiting on dry land
I'm not made for swimming
Can you understand?"

The sky was now darker as the sun had long set
And the lost baby zebra was beginning to fret
Together they crept towards the long grass
Willing and praying for the time soon to pass

Zebra kept searching the dark moonlit sky
Wishing that eagle would fly up right by
And bring them news
of what he had seen
And hopefully where his
mom and dad had been

"Shhhhhhh, what's that? I heard something!

It came from somewhere in the dark
I don't think it's a grunting sound from a hog
Or a throaty croak from a toad or a frog
It sounded more like a growl
Than a bark
From way out there, in the dark"

Suddenly zebra stopped dead in his tracks
For right behind the rhino's back
Stood a group of wild dogs – a hunting pack!

"Just ignore them and stay put
I'll kick up sand with my front foot
Then I'll charge them with my pointy horn
Pricking them quickly like a thorn"

With a yelp and growl and the occasional bark
The wild dogs ran off into the dark

And when they were nowhere to be seen
Down flew eagle
to tell where he'd been

The moon of the night had faded away
And the rays from the sun
now brought in the day

"There's a dazzle of zebra just over that hill
If you leave right now, they should be there still
On the way up, listen out for the sound
To help you find your way around"

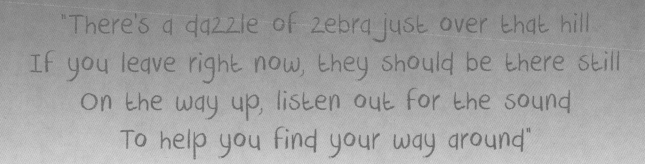

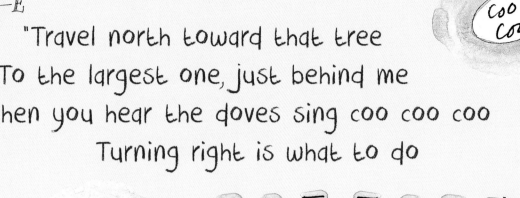

"Travel north toward that tree
To the largest one, just behind me
When you hear the doves sing coo coo coo
Turning right is what to do

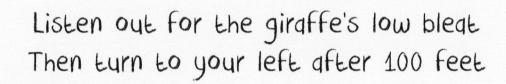

Listen out for the giraffe's low bleat
Then turn to your left after 100 feet

When you hear the sound
of hyena's laugh
You must turn right
and follow the path

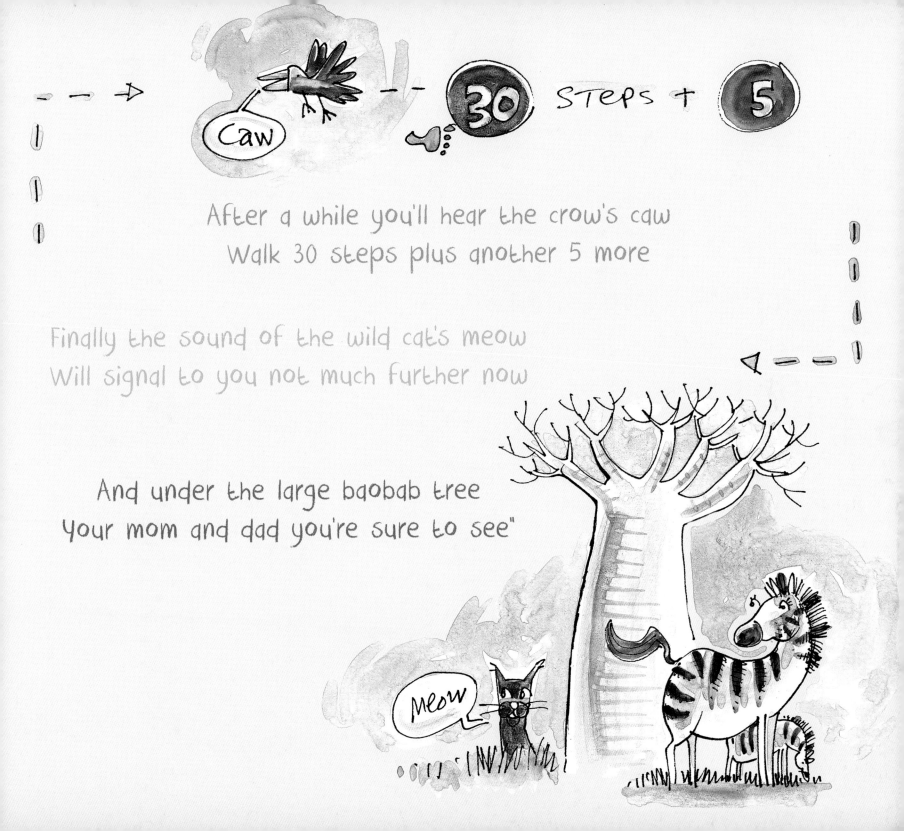

After a while you'll hear the crow's caw
Walk 30 steps plus another 5 more

Finally the sound of the wild cat's meow
Will signal to you not much further now

And under the large baobab tree
Your mom and dad you're sure to see"

"Rhino and eagle: a big THANKS to YOU!
I'd still be lost in the land of Kachoo
If it wasn't for help from the two of you"

"Goodbye," he said, before heading north in the morning light
Hoping he'd soon see his parents in sight

There at the tree he heard coo coo coo
Turning right is what I must do

Soon he heard the giraffe's low bleat
Now I turn left after 100 feet

Then he heard the hyena's laugh
I turn to the right
and follow the path

After a while he heard the crow's caw
What did he say?
Walk 30 steps plus another 5 more

Finally the sound of the wild cat's meow
Signalled to zebra not much further now

And, there, waiting under the baobab tree
Stood his mom, his dad, his whole family

"Mommy, daddy, I'm here at last!"

'How did you manage to find us so fast?"

"It's thanks to eagle and rhino, my friends"

"Hooray for them!
This day happily ends"

First published by Jacana Media (Pty) Ltd in 2012

10 Orange Street
Sunnyside
Auckland Park 2092
South Africa
(+27 11) 628-3200
www.jacana.co.za

In collaboration with 2sq Design (Pty) Ltd
© Text: Tina Scotford, 2012
© Illustrations: Frans Groenewald, 2012

ISBN 978-1-4314-0694-4

Editor: Dominique Herman
Designer: Jeannie Coetzee
Set in DK Crayon Crumble 22 pt
Job no. 001812
Printed by Tien Wah Press (Pte) Ltd

See a complete list of Jacana titles at www.jacana.co.za